MOUNTAIN MAGIC

MOUNTAIN MAGIC

VAN GREAVES

F

FRANCES LINCOLN LIMITED

PUBLISHERS

Frances Lincoln Ltd
4 Torriano Mews
Torriano Avenue
London NW5 2RZ
www.franceslincoln.com

Mountain Magic
Copyright © Frances Lincoln 2009
Text copyright © Van Greaves 2009
Photographs copyright © Van Greaves 2009

First Frances Lincoln edition: 2009

A catalogue record for this book is available from the British Library.

ISBN 978-0-7112-2858-0

Printed and bound in Singapore

9 8 7 6 5 4 3 2 1

PAGE 1
Buachaille Etive Mor reflected, Scottish Highlands
One of a series of shots that a superb dawn light allowed on this great Scottish peak.

PAGES 2–3
On the arete of Meall Garbh, Tarmachan Ridge, Scottish Highlands
Three climbers enjoy the fantastic winter conditions on this fine, though short arete, where the mountains seem to go on forever in the distance. Note Ben More and Stob Binnean on the left of the picture.

BELOW
Last light on rocks of Esk Pike, Lake District
The way the last rays of the sun caught the rocks aboard Esk Pike here was particularly attractive. It was then a task of looking for a compostion that arranged them neatly in their eliptical formation. The Langdale Pikes, Windermere and part of Bowfell form the background.

CONTENTS

INTRODUCTION

I recently experienced a dream trip: nine continuous days of 'Ansel Adams' skies in the Highlands of Scotland. The wind remained easterly, the atmosphere pristine, and white fluffy cumulous clouds decorated clear blue skies. The mornings and evenings were full of drama and colour, and I was so busy taking photographs that I wouldn't have been surprised if I had suffered from repetitive strain injury in my camera hand. The chill in the air, despite being dry enough to crack my fingers, simply did not matter as I enjoyed a veritable photographic spree.

Often I have come back from a three-week trip to the American West with enough good photographs that would have required maybe six months equivalent time on these islands, such is the inclement weather conditions that usually prevail. Add to this the fact that British mountains attract the worst of this weather, and it becomes clear that obtaining a collection of photographs depicting them is, on the surface at least, a daunting task.

The only type of collection I would be satisfied with on such a subject is a long-term one, and the earliest picture in this book is forty years old, although the majority were taken over the last twenty years.

I drew and painted pictures of mountains before I ever saw one. From my youth, I was far more fascinated by maps, contours and my father's illustrated book, Romantic Britain (particularly the sections on Wales, Lake District and Scottish Highlands), than I was by any work of fiction. I copied the monochrome mountain pictures out of the book and painted them in my own colours. A piece of Snowdon rock lay on the mantlepiece from my parents' trip to the summit by train, and it served to fire my imagination because they said it was in the cloud at the time. A coach trip to Snowdonia via the Llanberis Pass saw me gape upwards in awe at the tiny figures perched on cliffs such as Dinas Mot and Dinas Cromlech.

Four years later at the age of eighteen, I satisfied my in-built free spirit and cycled to Snowdonia, climbing Moel Siabod, the Glyders and Snowdon. I took a Kodak Brownie 127 camera and began photographing mountains.

Photography has been a natural metamorphosis. I could have retained and developed my talent for the pencil or the brush, but instead I turned to the camera. Nothing in the world gives me more pleasure than photographing landscapes, and no landscape is grander than our British mountains.

If you measure the impact of world mountains by height alone, then British mountains would be insignificant. Everest is about twice the height in metres as Ben Nevis, our highest mountain, is measured in feet! However, apart from the altitude, the many technical problems encountered for example on 'The Ben' in winter, are at least comparable to those met on an eight thousand metre peak.

The greater ranges, however, are the domain of the fittest, toughest and most technically gifted climbers in the world, but many of these have been British, their skills honed on the mountains of their homeland. Somehow, our little mountains contain their own grandeur, their own toughness. And they also photograph on a par with the greater ranges.

There seems to be a greater range of light and atmospheric conditions in Britain than can be captured by a photographer in the greater ranges, such as the Himalaya North America, the Alps and Scandinavia. The view I saw from Auli Meadows, near Josimath, in the Garwhal Himalayas, which mountaineer Frank Smythe described as the best in the Himalayas, was stunning. However, I cannot say it moved me any more than looking from a pristine Scottish winter mountain across the vast Highland panorama looking like an ocean crested with the white waves represented by the peaks.

One of the differences of photographing in Scotland in particular is the constant proximity of water. The inundation of the landscape by sea and freshwater lochs adds a whole new dimension, whether you look up from the loch side to a mountain, or from a mountain down to the shimmering sheets of water below. Our Cumbrian mountains are also blessed with lakes; Wales, less so, but all our mountain regions have lochans (in Scotland), tarns (in Lakeland), and llyns (in Wales). These beautiful sheets of water decorate former glaciated

Sun Spectre from Snowdon, Snowdonia

I was standing just beneath Snowdon summit one early morning in late August. The sun had just risen above the cloud bank which is seen behind the Mymbyr lakes, near Capel Curig. The water acted as a mirror at the perfect angle to beam the sun's reflected disc towards the camera. This reflection was further enhanced by passing through a thin veil of mist, causing the concentric rings of the spectrum around it. It was a one-off experience, unlikely ever to be repeated.

hollows, some support soaring rock buttresses frequented by climbers. From my own experience, I am convinced they are as rewarding photographically as anywhere in the world.

My mountain photography learning curve has been long and it still continues. While many of my mountaineering peers have other agendas – like ticking off Munros, 'Corbetts' and even the lesser heights called 'Grahams' their heads eternally glued to the ground in a quest to cover miles or gain tops – I might be found stuck in one spot, just waiting for the light. That need for a challenge in the mountains was played out long ago during my younger days.

Today I will often be found observing my surroundings, waiting for a fleeting moment of light on a mountainside. The sweat in gaining my position might now be dampening my skin, making me feel colder by the minute. But this is over-ruled by my concentration to press that camera shutter, sometimes not at all, or sometimes only once or twice over a fleeting moment, but at other times in a feast of rewarding images.

Mountain photography is an unsociable practice. I invariably find myself alone. Either my climbing colleagues have moved on to other objectives, or they are simply not there and I am on my own. This is because the best photographic times of day often coincide with normal daytime routines, such as getting up, breakfast, or evening

meals. But my abstinence of these has been rewarded with some of the best light and moments our mountains have to offer. Frankly, remembering my recent Scottish trip, I found myself in a kind of photographic heaven.

I keep to the 35mm format, though I have tried medium and large. I could not have captured successfully the moment revealed by 'Summit Light, Carn Mor Dearg,' (p.8) for instance, on any other format. I like the immediacy of the 35mm format.

Most of the images in this book have come from using Nikon cameras and, over the last few years, digital imaging has replaced my former use of film. My pictures may be described from record to pictorial, but I am always conscious of design in any photographic composition. Pre-knowledge of weather, terrain, light possibilities, position of the sun, and use of camera exposures and other operations are necessities, but always, when successful pictures are gained, governed by a certain amount of luck.

I hope I have captured a comprehensive variety of British mountain images that give the reader as much pleasure in looking at them as I have had taking them, and that they truly reveal that our hills have that 'Mountain Magic.'

Van Greaves, May 2008

Summit Light, Carn Mor Dearg, Ben Nevis, Scottish Highlands

The task of tackling the classic Ben Nevis circuit via the Carn Mor Dearg arete in winter was hampered by some fierce squalls, punctuated by extremely brief spells of sunlight. Having crossed the ridge and somewhere near the abseil poles, I braced myself against a boss of snow and tried to catch one of these on film. Seeing the light coming, I put the camera onto continuous frame mode, no more than three frames per second. The speed of the light only enabled three shots, and the middle one was the only one to catch a perfect triangle of light on Carn Mor Dearg. Figures can be seen on the ridge battling the 50-foot sprays of spindrift.

Dawn light, Buachaille Etive Mor, Glencoe, Scottish Highlands
Mountain photography is often a gamble of balancing anticipated good weather conditions against driving distance. I drove overnight from the Midlands to Rannoch Moor, bedded down in the car and hoped for a dawn on one of Britain's most iconic mountains. Nature smiled on me on this occasion, and, from just along the river by the girder bridge, I got a series of shots of dawn light gradually illuminating the Buchaille, first from its summit tip and slowly, the whole of the rest of the mountain. Although I later got a few shots in Glencoe, the downside was I was travelling north to Torridon, and over the next eight days only managed about three meaningful photographs, which obviates the need to describe the weather which followed.

Cloudspill, Corn Du, Brecon Beacons

The sun was included as the cloud spilled over the edge of Corn Du, in the central Brecon Beacons. This star-like effect was gained by using a closed-down aperture of f22 with careful consideration to the exposure, particularly as snow scenes can be tricky in this situation. If in doubt, don't be afraid of bracketing digital frames if possible. If using normal film, as here, take three shots in third of a stop increments from normal to a third or two thirds or even a full stop below the normal reading.

Summit Silhouette, Snowdon, Snowdonia

This is an early image taken on Agfa slide film, which always gave a grainy result, even at 100 ASA. My female partner is seen in silhouette looking at Snowdon from Crib y Ddysgl. It was a December day with conditions of temperature inversion. From an early stage in my photography, I seldom used a figure as dominant as this in a mountain image, unless I was taking a snap or record shot of a companion which would interest only those personally involved or relatives and friends. However, in this case, the wind had wisped the cloud up and over the ridge we were standing on, and also the hair of my companion, whose stance seems to be of an observer of this wonderful weather phenomena. Somehow, the anonymous silhouetted figure gives a human dimension to the mountain as do the tiny figures of walkers on the summit ridge of Snowdon beyond.

First Light, Robinson and High Stile Ridge, Lake District
This is probably the most vivid dawn light I have ever seen on a British mountain. A photographer prays for this colour, but the chances are rare that it will reach this level of intensity.

Red sky from Foel Grach, Snowdonia

I had planned to climb Pen yr Ole Wen from Ogwen, walk over Carnedd Dafydd and continue to Carnedd Llewelyn where I would bivouac. A balmy July afternoon and a fair forecast turned on its head and I found myself wandering the ridge in increasing mist. A few breaks occurred over The Black Ladders, but it began to get damp and cold. Decision time was on Carnedd Llewelyn. I would not risk a bivouac in the open, but would continue to the Foel Grach mountain refuge, where, simple shelter though it is, protection is gained from the elements. At least I might get a chance of pictures the following morning. I located the refuge, almost hewn into the rock, and went inside to lay down my sleeping bag in the approaching light of evening. I then stepped outside, and the cloud suddenly lifted to reveal a fantastic sky. Taking no chances with finding a carefully selected foreground, I decided to keep this feature low and make the wonderful sky the dominating feature of several exposures, resulting in this one.

Wastwater Screes, Lake District

An autumn visit to Wastwater yielded plenty of images during a good spell
of weather. The light might have been a degree or two stronger as I looked
across at the screes in the late afternoon, but it still allowed a short telephoto
shot across the lake to compose the pattern seen here, with a small strip of
water at its base. The fans of the screes are seen to good advantage.

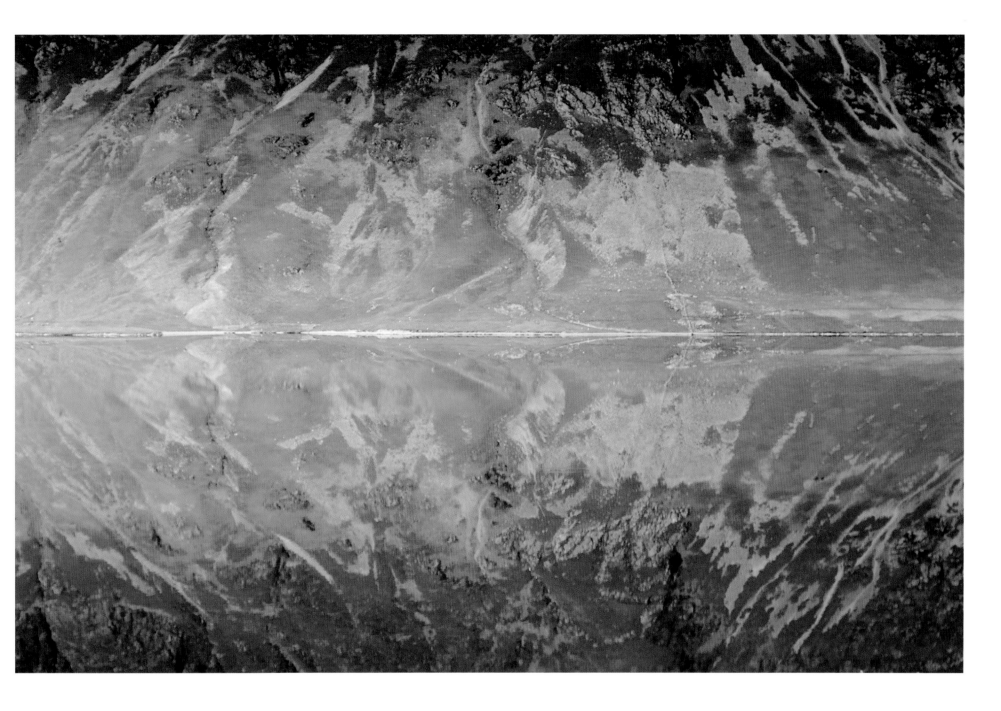

Melbreak Screes reflected in Crummock Water, Lake District
Complimenting the previous image, this one was taken on an early
summer's morning along the shores of Crummock Water. It allowed a
reflection of the screes in the calm lake. Note the major shift in vegetation
colour between the seasons in the resulting two photographs.

Cuillin Summits from Sgumain/Alasdair Ridge, Skye

Perhaps the figure is a bit posed, but this was in my novice photographic days. She is however nicely positioned and relaxed in her classic mountain surroundings. While the mainland was plagued with cloud, Skye was gratefully free of it, and we enjoyed the rarity of several good days on the island. On this occasion we did the Round of Coire Laggan.

Looking down onto Cuillin Main Ridge including Sgurr Mhic Coinnich from Sgurr Alasdair, Skye

The tiny figures make the shot as they progress towards Sgurr Mhic Coinnich, beyond the intervening lump on the ridge. Sgurr Mhic Coinnich is defined by the rising diagonal of Hart's (or Collie's) Ledge. I deliberately contained the whole rocky scene without the sky, because if it had been included, it would have made the climbers even smaller and possibly distracted from the scene by being too much in contrast to the sombre colours of the rocky environment.

Ridge Lines, Meall Corranaich, Tayside, Scottish Highlands

Often, particularly in the Highlands, the fickle British weather interferes with the views of the summits. However in this example, as the cloud rolled in over Meall Corranaich's summit, there was sufficient light from the Arctic conditions to allow me to compose a play on lines making a geometrical zig-zag design across the picture, then turning upwards towards an unseen summit on the right. This type of picture comes instinctively, both from observation and prior knowledge of what will work under inclement conditions. When light under many circumstances might be considered 'flat,' snow will reflect so much more back to the camera than bare rock will under the same conditions.

Mists over Ogwen, Snowdonia

Similar to the last picture, while making an ascent of Y Garn via the right hand of the two distinctive ridges seen from Ogwen or Llyn Idwal and above Llyn Clyd, I noticed the mists creating a veil across the scene. The temptation would have been to wait for these to lift and give a factual interpretation of the retrospective mountain landscape, accentuated by Tryfan and Llyn Ogwen. I took a couple of pictures while the mists prevailed, giving this resultant ethereal effect.

PAGE 20–21

Castlerigg Stone Circle and Blencathra, Lake District

The standing stones of the Castlerigg stone circle are situated in a field on top of a flat hill outside Keswick. The megalithic monument is 5000 years old, and the stones are said to reflect features in the surrounding landscape. They may also indicate astronomical alignments. I have made several visits to the site, but never come away with a definitive picture. This image shows the dramatic light which hung around the area when much of Lakeland's peaks were under cloud. The sunlight came in from a perfect angle on the stones, where behind, the brooding bulk of Blencathra, one of Cumbria's finest mountains, made the perfect backcloth.

LEFT

Evil Eye, Upper Tor, Kinder Scout, High Peak, Derbyshire

I haven't seen a published photograph showing what appears to be a demonic face or gargoyle-like resemblance of this rock of Upper Tor, perched as it is overlooking the upper reaches of Edale. Any photographer looking for something other than straight landscapes would do well to investigate the innumerable fascinating rocks which form the surrounds of the Pennine Way on Kinder Scout.

RIGHT

Pig-like rock, Crowden Tower, Kinder Scout, Peak District

Eons of weathering have sculptured the gritstone rocks on the summits of the Pennines, none more so than in this area, where some shapes take on those of animals. In fact, The Woolpacks on the southern slopes of Kinder Scout are also known as Whipsnade and the Mushroom Garden. Thousands of walkers pass this rock without ever noticing it. It is only revealed if they venture off the path to view its opposite (hidden) face.

Langdale Pikes Recession, Lake District

Taken near Bowfell, I was keen to illustrate the Pikes and atmospheric conditions in *contra jour* (against the light) conditions. Here, shapes are defined without detail in them due to the varying layers of shade on the receding features. The cloud and sky were held in by the use of a graduated grey filter. While the eye can adjust to the different exposures between land and sky densities, neither film nor digital imaging can achieve the same without artifical assistance. This is not meant to be a photographic manual, but if you have an SLR in the mountains, find out about the different grad-grey filters there are, (along with their respective holders to fit on your lenses) to balance your exposures as mentioned above.

Mountain recession from Cnicht, Snowdonia
This is a sister shot to the previous one on the Langdale Pikes (left). I have used the diagonal sweeps of the mountain ridges from top left to bottom right to enhance the composition. To achieve this, I have cropped the full 35mm image, not a regular habit but used where it improves the result. The near base of the slopes of the Moelwyns seemed far too dominant in full format. Also, even though I did my best to prevent 'flare,' it began to creep in on the bottom part of the original image, and cropping eliminated this. The distant ridge is Cadair Idris.

Marsco and reflected cloud, Skye
Taken near Sligachan, the cloud and the streak of similar coloured light on Marsco are the makings of the image. There is no secret in the fact that it was again early morning and the elements were in my favour.

Stac Pollaidh from Loch Cail an Uidhean, Scottish Highlands

The tiny road from Lochinver bounding Inverpolly Forest is enchanting in its tantalising views of the isolated peaks of this stunning area. Photography is like a drug, with the addictive quest to always achieve even better pictures. However, this photograph taken early in the morning satisfies me in the fact that I could hardly return to the location and come up with anything better. The balance of compositional elements and the play of contrasting colours, particularly between the yellow gorse, the blue loch and the pink cloud hovering over the mountain, make this a pleasing image.

Rhinog Fawr from Llyn Cwm Hosan, Snowdonia

This is a lovely, lonely spot, a few hundred feet above the Bwlch Drws Ardudwy, a remote pass in itself. The curving anticline of the strata of Rhinog Fawr is illustrated to good advantage. It is hard to realise that the land here at one time was higher than Snowdon, which is now a full 1,100 feet higher than Rhinog Fawr, but situated on a syncline. Essentially, this is a record shot under factual lighting, but wherever I find this light, I always try to make the best of it.

Snowdon from Llyn Padarn, Snowdonia

Taken on a September evening when the angle of the sun painted pleasing warm colours both on the shoreline reeds and the mountain beyond, which is topped by attractive cloud. The viewpoint has often been photographed, but I was in the right place at the right time to make a slightly more compelling image, particularly when a swan chose to swim across the lake and its reflection was cast both in the water and inside the reflection of the mountain.

Cloud and light over Sgurr Nan Gillean, Skye
The best known photographic angle on the mountain from Sligachan is usually just down the road from this spot, using the river and/or its bridge as foreground. But I decided to find a different foreground by using this lochan, which gave a reflection of the mountain.

PAGE 30–31
Loch Na Stainge & Blackmount (Stob a' Choire Odhair) in light, Scottish Highlands
This and the next image are easily-gained locations for the photographer. You don't need mountaineering skills or even to walk very far, because the view is virtually by the roadside. The secret is to be out early, and that is tied up with the weather forecast and luck with light. I drove from Tyndrum at 5am onto Rannoch Moor and shots that had evaded me for years over several crossings of this tremendous wilderness were at last captured. There was strong early sunshine beneath some stunning cloud formations over The Blackmount. The rest was down to choice of composition, focal length of lens, exposure and filters.

Rannoch Moor, (Blackmount from Lochan na h-Achlaise), Scottish Highlands
This is another view which has been photographed profusely. None of my
photographic club members are mountaineers and few are even walkers, but like
hundreds of societies (plus innumerable photographers up and down the country),
they know this view. My aim if I photograph a 'done to death scene' is to do it in
quality light and conditions. The weather was in the process of change from low
pressure to high, and the consequent dawn break-up in what was previously a cloudy
night gave me numerous images of this wild scene, just yards from the A82. I could
have chosen any one of them, such was the dramatic light and sky. I had intended to
photograph Ben Lui that morning, but it had remained under cloud cover and looked
in no mood to reveal itself.

The development of the cloud formation is seen in this alternative
image from the same area as the photograph opposite.

Whiteless Pike, Wandope & Crag Hill, Lake District

Driving up the Newlands Pass, I saw that by careful composition I had two repeating diagonals going from bottom left to right in the bottom half of the picture, then three repeating diagonals, from the shadow and the two mountain ridges going upwards and opposite from right to left in the upper part. Two fluffy clouds were drifting by conveniently in the sky to complete the scene.

Gearr Aonach & Aonach Dubh, Glencoe, Scottish Highlands

On the bend in the pass of Glencoe near the waterfalls and on the opposite side of the road, I climbed a shallow gully to reach a flat perch to look for a photographic opportunity. Typically, in August, a promising start to the day was beginning to change as cloud built up from the southwest. The low angle and proximity to the soaring Three Sisters on the opposite side of the glen forced me to look for a meaningful telephoto shot, and this one saw passing light on the cliffs of Gearr Aonach contrasting well with the repeated shape of Aonach Dubh in dark shadow.

Limestone Jigsaw, Southerscales, Yorkshire Dales

Britain is blessed with so many variations in landscape, a fine example being the limestone pavements of North Yorkshire. If you know where to park on the Ingleton to Hawes road, it is not a major undertaking to reach arguably the best pavements there are, at Southerscales. With a walk of a mere mile and an easy ascent, you will be captivated when arriving at the flat broken pavement, with the clints divided by narrow crevices which are known as grykes stretching across acres of limestone beneath Ingleborough. This was a November shot after rain, where I managed to compose this lovely interlinking pattern. It is worth noting that although at over 1,200 feet above sea level, the grykes form a micro-climate within which numerous plants grow, including rare ferns and even marsh marigolds in Spring.

Winter Mosaic, Red Tarn, Helvellyn, Lake District

On a Sunday coach trip with the West Bromwich Mountaineering Club to Thirlmere, I climbed Brown Pike and headed for Helvellyn's summit. It was a typical squally March day. With the cloud keeping the sun at bay, I saw Red Tarn some 700 feet below. Its ice cover was breaking up into a wonderful mosaic-like pattern, but without the light to accentuate it. With my fellow climbers, I headed to the large walled shelter in the shape of a cross some yards below the summit where, after about 15 minutes and a bite to eat, my colleagues took off for Lower Man. Doggedly, I sat at the cairn for an hour waiting for the sunlight, if only for a brief spell, to allow me to photograph the lake from above. Finally, almost at the end of my patience and resistance to the cold, I dashed to the summit, risked death with a cornice and eventually got some sunlight over the lake, with an angle and pattern I have not witnessed since.

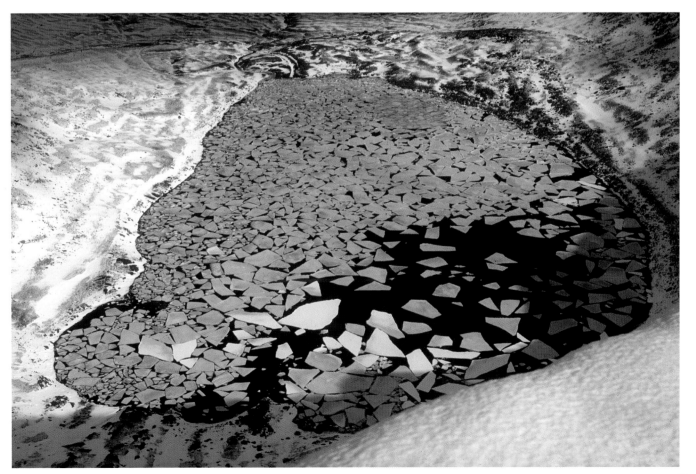

Dawn Wedge over Scafells from Bowfell, Lake District

This and the following photograph illustrate the wonderful turn of light that is possible during what is sometimes labelled as 'the magic hour' – one hour either side of dawn or dusk. I fondly remember the bivouac my son and I had between Esk Pike and Bowfell on this stunning August day. We had hiked out of Langdale via Mickleden and Rossett Ghyll, starting at 5pm. The fantastic thing about enjoying an overnight stop in the mountains is the lack of other people, who pass us going down while we ascend, and miss out on the tremendous experience of a sunset or sunrise at altitude. Before sunrise, on an unpolluted night such as this and under a very Milky Way, the sky, approximately 180 degrees opposite to where the sun will rise, glows pink, as sunlight reflects off particles in the upper atmosphere. This is a phenomena which can be seen at any altitude, but at height and against a backcloth of England's highest peaks, it becomes something else in intensity. I used a graduated grey filter to hold the lighter sky colours in some balance with the darker colours of the rocks and mountains.

Scafells at sunrise from Bowfell, Lake District
This second image is in sequence from the first one, where the dawn wedge had disappeared to be replaced by the first (almost orange) rays of light on the summit rocks of Bowfell and the Scafells beyond.

Figures on Crib Goch, Snowdonia

An early start on the Snowdon Horseshoe had beaten the crowds. Looking back from somewhere on Crib y Ddysgl, I saw the first of these crowds in procession traversing Crib Goch. I also noticed via my telephoto lens that I could isolate the almost repeating shapes of Crib Goch with the peak of Moel Siabod behind.

Figures on Hart's Ledge (aka Collie's Ledge)
on Sgurr Mhic Coinnich, Skye
The angle of view complete with the tiny figures gives a
greater sense of exposure than is actually experienced
on this traverse. This is not to detract from the climbers'
position on this rugged Cuillin peak, which is exciting and
always commands respect.

Lochan a' Choire and Creag Meagaidh, Scottish Highlands

One of the largest precipices in Scotland draws the eye after turning the corner of the woods of Coill a' Choire. Its cliffs are a rock climber's playground, but more impressively, when hard winter conditions prevail, both the buttresses and gullies offer some of Scotland's finest ice climbs. The small tarn of Lochan a' Choire is a fitting place to study this magnificent arena, perhaps resting for a bite to eat before tackling a climb, or less technically going up 'The Window,' the declivity seen on the right, to battle above with the slopes that guard the summit, broad and exposed to the elements. Winter sunlight does not fall often into this amphitheatre, but again, the reflection of light off ice and snow gave this pleasing exposure. The frozen rock in the ice of the tarn gives an all-important foreground to the great bastion behind.

South Top, Beinn a' Chaorainn, Scottish Highlands
There was plenty of snow, but it was altogether too soft, and it was a real toil to get to the two tops of this mountain from Roughburn on Loch Moy. This would not have been a good day to tackle technically steep slopes, due to the risk of avalanche. But despite the poor conditions underfoot, good photographic conditions prevailed. I was able to get this image with lots of spindrift billowing up the mountainside. This seems to raise the picture beyond a simple record shot, and enhance the harshness of the environment.

Tryfan from Llyn Caseg-ffraith, Snowdonia
It is always exciting when sunlight bathes an interesting foreground while the
background, in this case, Tryfan, is dramatised under dark clouds. This was an
autumn shot, and makes a fascinating comparison to the winter shot which follows.

Tryfan in winter raiment, Snowdonia

In the early months of 1986, even the road where I lived was frozen for most of the month of February. An ascent of the Glyders from the A5 at Gwern-y-Gof-Isaf farm up Braich y Ddeugwm brought us to Llyn Caseg-ffraith... but we couldn't see it under the inundation of snow and ice. I have never seen Tryfan so plastered in snow and ice, and possibly will never do so again. The steep rock buttresses above the Heather Terrace were all but covered in a freezing white cloak. This day led to several other pictures which would be hard to repeat today due to global warming.

Young Red Deer & Sgurr Mor, Knoydart, Scottish Highlands

I am not a wildlife photographer. Landscape is hard enough without sitting in a hide for hours on end to obtain pictures of fauna. However, I could not pass up this chance to snap one of Britain's most noble creatures. An October walk along Loch Quoich saw plenty of red deer gathering for the rut. This young stag was keeping away from the dominant males, apparently unready for a fight. Like it or not, these animals are managed, and this one probably belonged to the Kinlochourn Estate.

Ptarmigan in summer plumage, Scottish Highlands

I was returning to the Bealach Na Ba from a walk over the rough country to Beinn Bhan in Applecross when I suddenly saw this example of one of Scotland's loveliest birds. It was only about 10 metres away and it made sure it got out of my way, (or so it thought) behind a big boulder on a bluff. I took time to change my standard camera lens for my telephoto zoom lens and creep around the bluff in the hope that I would find the bird. Sure enough, there it was, and this is the result. Note how the bird's plumage is in harmony with its summer surrounds. It becomes white in winter.

Rowan & the High Stile ridge, Buttermere, Lake District

This twisted rowan tree is at the Gatesgarth end of Buttermere. Early one
June morning, I found it catching a perfect spotlight, and I used it to point
down towards the becalmed lake, with the High Stile ridge reflected beyond.
I cannot emphasise enough how important it is to get out early in the
mountains for picture-taking particularly before the crowds arrive.

Looking down Langdale
Yes, there is another 'Langdale' in the Howgill Fells. The atmosphere was clear, allowing a view through the valley across the Vale of Eden to the snow-covered High Pennines, where it is possible to pick out Cross Fell, the highest top in the Pennines and the radar dome on Little Dun Fell. The one spur, left, flanking the valley was perfectly shaded by cloud, which helped give depth to the composition.

Haystacks reflected in Buttermere, Lake District
This shot was taken on the same morning as the previous picture and a little further on, with the lovely crags of Haystacks reflected in the millpond that was Buttermere.

Foinaven, Scottish Highlands
One of Britain's most northerly mountains, 911m/2,980ft Foinaven reveals itself from numerous positions along the wild stretches of the A838 in Sutherland. A pristine day gives a good result, with the lochan proving a useful foreground.

A view of Arkle from River Laxford, Scottish Highlands
Foinaven's neighbour, Arkle, is exactly 400 feet lower than its rival, but none the less imposing. Here, the River Laxford provides a useful lead-in to the mountain.

Snow Lines, towards Cribyn, Brecon Beacons

Some may question global warming, but this photograph is testament to the harder winters of not so many years ago. The descent from Pen y Fan via Cefn Cwn Llwch is a pleasant, broad ridge in summer, but was transformed here by a considerable snowfall, sculptured by wind into furrows which lead the eye to the fine pyramid of Cribyn across Cwm Llwch.

Jet Tracks above Bowfell, Lake District
Glaramara could not be considered a classic mountain such as Great Gable, but it is beautifully decorated with tarns and rocky bluffs. It also yields fine views of many other Lakeland mountains. A thin path traverses the mountain towards Allen Crags, but not all the tarns are visible from it. This particular one is off-track, hemmed in an amphitheatre of rocks and revealing Bowfell beyond, its summit reflected in the still water. I normally do not like the inclusion of modern day jet trails in otherwise timeless pictures, but on this occasion very early in the day, the busy trans-Atlantic air traffic created a zig-zag pattern which enhanced the picture in an unusual way.

Skiddaw from Littledale Edge, Lake District

Littledale Edge is a connecting ridge on the Dale Head-Robinson traverse, and early on an August morning I saw this view from the edge north to Skiddaw. What made it attractive to me were the various layers of land each creating their own shape and tone, leading towards the distant mountain bulk.

Mosedale & Pillar from Lingmell, Lake District

Climbing Lingmell from Wasdale in autumn revealed this fine overlook of Wasdale Head, Mosedale, the valley beyond the buildings and Pillar. Cloud was moving constantly, so I waited for an opportune moment to grab this image where the juxtaposition of light, shade, cloud and sky was optimal.

Evening Light, Great Gable, Lake District

This autumn shot was taken just by the wall to Wasdale church, where the graded path heads for Sty Head Pass under the flanks of Great Gable. I did not stray from Wasdale for several days because of a particular weather pattern. Beyond Gable to the east, cloud had drifted in from the North Sea and lodged itself over many of the eastern fells, but the wall of England's highest mountains was acting as a barrier, keeping generally sunny weather to the west. I was attracted to the light and shadow patterns illuminating the mountain.

Evening Light, Pen-y-ghent, Yorkshire Dales

Another mountain lit by evening light. The southern aspect of Pen-y-ghent had been enduring cloudy weather, but looking west towards Morecambe Bay, I could see that a bank of cloud was concealing the sun. With luck, if the cloud bank stayed at a constant level, or even drifted towards me, I could see that if I hung around, the sun would dip low enough to light Pen-y-ghent. After a 45-minute wait, it finally happened. Not only that, but the cloud over the mountain was breaking and revealing a cobalt blue sky. So relieved that this had happened, I shot off a whole roll of film!

Ladhar Bheinn from Stob a' Choire Odhair, Knoydart, Scottish Highlands

Readers will recall there is another mountain called Stob a' Choire Odhair some miles south on Rannoch Moor. Whereas the view of the Rannoch Moor peak was taken from the roadside, this one had to be hard fought for. It was a six to seven mile hike into Knoydart's interior, carrying full pack and rations, from Kinlochourn to the bothy at Barisdale. Not only that, I had to carry an ice axe and crampons as extra safety gear. I chose my four-season boots in case I had to wear crampons, but they ended up severely blistering my heels. In an eight-mile slog the next day, I climbed Ladhar Bheinn alone in superb weather, via Coire Dhorrcail and the stiff slopes of Stob a' Choire Odhair, a satellite to Ladhar Bheinn which turns into a real 'horn' of a mountain. I didn't need the crampons, but the airy, steep ridge of my first top contained every kind of snow condition. Some areas were crisp and hard; some were hard and soft over a few steps, and some were very soft and dangerous. I decided not to do the circuit due to my blisters, fatigue and the dodgy snow conditions, and returned the same way, retracing my footsteps in the virgin snow.

The Rough Bounds of Knoydart, Scottish Highlands

Just three days into my April Scottish sojourn, I realised that I had hit on some exceptional weather, so I set off for Knoydart as my first objective. I desperately wanted some pictures from there, and was not going for any other reason. This is the reward for my efforts. I do not claim exceptional light and atmospherics, but I do claim my pictures of a pristine Knoydart are not often seen by its visitors. Joe Williams of Kinlochourn Farm told me that there had been 51 inches of rain so far that year, prior to this fine spell. It was simply a privilege to see the Rough Bounds so clearly and precisely presented. Note among Knoydart's numerous peaks, Luinne Bheinn and Sgurr na Ciche, the latter to the right.

From Thornthwaite Crag to Brothers Water, Lake District

Sometimes I look at a grand landscape and guage how I might condense it. Instead of taking in a wide angle view of this scene to include much more mountain and sky, I chose to fit in Brothers Water and part of Ullswater behind, simply because there was a pleasant interplay of light and shade throughout the composition, which leads nicely through from foreground to background.

Dawn light on Craig Cywarch from Hengwm, Snowdonia

In fine weather in December, the first rays of the sun catch the fine buttresses of Craig Cywarch. This valley was reachable in a day for me from my home with an early start, when empty roads aided arrival via Dinas Mawddwy into Cwm Cywarch for a torchlight start up Hengwm, an impressive 'V' cut valley which gives access to the Aran ridge. Some way up the ascent I stopped, turned around and erected the tripod to take varying focal length views of the crag as it caught the light. The shot I liked was this one, where the composition is compressed and the pink light on the rocks is at its maximum, contrasting nicely with the nearer green slopes.

Light on Lingmell Crag, Lake District

An ascent of Scafell Pike from Wasdale was chosen via Lingmell, where this view from its summit shows the detached Lingmell Crag in front, with Sty Head Tarn and Borrowdale behind. There was this lovely play of light on Lingmell Crag, and it gave me the opportunity to photograph in portrait rather than landscape, mode.

Pencoed Pillar, Craig Cau, Cadair Idris

In the crossing of Craig Cau on the Minffordd Path of Cadair Idris, a gully reveals the rock bastion of the Pencoed Pillar on top of which a tiny figure stands. The buttress gives a 'hard very severe' rock climb in obvious steep and spectacular surroundings above Llyn Cau.

On Bannau Sir Gaer, Brecon Beacons

The January light was low and the sky was brooding as I made a circuit of the Carmarthen Fans. I thought I would see no one until some walkers appeared on the skyline. I yelled across the void for them to walk nearer to the edge, and fortunately, they heard me and realised what I was up to. They duly obliged and the overall result was pleasing, particularly the scale of the climbers against the sandstone scarp of the mountain.

Fellsman's Light (above Ullswater), Lake District

Descending St. Sunday Crag, I noticed a patch of light clinging to a rocky outcrop down the fell. I urged one of my companions who was wearing a red cagoule to hurry down to the outcrop and climb on it. The rest was down to the light and the choice of framing, which deliberately did not include the sky but did include the subtle russets of a Lakeland autumn, and part of Ullswater below.

Yewbarrow & Wastwater, Lake District

Because Great Gable was cloud-capped on this autumn morning, I selected Yewbarrow on its own for this picture. Its summit was clear with attractive clouds above, both of which were reflected in the lake.

Snowdon Horseshoe reflected, Snowdonia
On an August morning at about 7am, I came upon the Mymbyr Lakes to find them calm and reflecting the Snowdon Horseshoe, beautifully graced with cloud. The result has an ethereal, painting-like quality to it, an effect, even though I have passed here on countless occasions, I've never seen repeated.

Early morning, Eastern Fells, Lake District

I started out from Pooley Bridge at about 4.30 on a July morning to walk the long broad ridge towards High Raise. There are several tops over 2000 feet on the way including Load Pot Hill, from which this picture was taken. The green grasses and the distant fells, of which Fairfield and Helvellyn are prominent, were decorated by attractive dappled clouds.

Cairngorms from Loch Morlich
A hard winter saw Loch Morlich frozen over, and a setting sun gave a delicate pink light on the mountains. Aesthetically, I might wish that the harsh line of the conifer plantation could be omitted.

Icy molars, Glyder Fach, Snowdonia
This image was taken during February, 1986, under hard winter conditions close by the top of Bristly Ridge. The cloud seemed to be rotating from the vertical to the right above the coatings of ice, snow and frost on the rocks. The cloud is shaped like the head of a sperm whale.

Hard Winter, Glyder Plateau, Snowdonia
The Glyder plateau is a photographer's paradise at any time under good conditions. Its rock formations are unique in style to British mountains, and when plastered in snow as here, in a shot taken the same day as the previous photograph, it was dramatised by a weather front creeping in, gave a brooding sky, and made this particular winter experience something of a one-off.

PAGE 70–71
Cairn Toul, Angel's Peak, Braeriach and the Lochaber Mountains from Ben Macdui, Cairngorms
Factual though this shot is, I couldn't have wished for better winter conditions and clarity of atmosphere from one of Scotland's greatest tops. Ben Nevis can be seen in the distance.

Y Garn reflected in Llyn y Cwn, Snowdonia

Llyn y Cwn (the Lake of the Dogs), lies beneath the scree slopes of
Glyder Fawr and gives a natural foreground to Y Garn. This calm
summer's morning, with the rich green of fresh new grasses, saw the
lake's surface very still, allowing a fine reflection of the mountain.

At Angle Tarn (Patterdale) Looking at Helvellyn group, Lake District
A pristine summer's morning gave this fresh-looking result. Angle Tarn is seen from above in its beautiful setting with a solitary figure for scale. Beyond the Helvellyn group paints an attractive skyline. Note there is another 'Angle Tarn' beneath Esk Pike in the Central Fells.

Southerscales & Ingleborough, Yorkshire Dales
The superb limestone pavements beneath Ingleborough (once thought to be the highest mountain in England), are best seen in late evening in spring or summer.

Whernside from Southerscales, Yorkshire Dales
The wintery light is low to the west and gives good relief to the limestone clints and grykes beneath Ingleborough. The wind-sculptured hawthorn tree adds foreground interest, with the whaleback of Whernside and clouds above completing the wild scene.

Along the Crib Goch Ridge
This classic view of the illustrative kind shows two walkers negotiating the beginning of one of the finest aretes in Britain, with Snowdon (Yr Wydffa) beyond. Early morning light gives good relief to the rocky landscape.

Along Quinag, Northwest Scottish Highlands
An early sprinkling of (October) snow gave the mountain added decoration. It is a sporting, undulating climb over various tops with great views out to sea, as depicted here.

Beinn Dearg from Coire Dubh, Scottish Highlands
Poor Torridonian weather forced a lower level trip into Coire Dubh between Liathach and Ben Eighe. During a very brief spell of sunshine, I grabbed some pictures of Ben Dearg at a tiny lochan, almost on top of the corrie. The vegetation points the way towards this mountain, which is a borderline Munro at just under 3,000 feet.

North along the Rhinogs from Rhinog Fach, Snowdonia
The anticline of Rhinog Fawr is seen to good effect as the view extends to Snowdon, clearly standing out on the horizon, over the northern Rhinogs, a very rough, rocky and heathery location.

Scafell Mood, Lake District

As I drove for the first time over the Ulpha Fell road, I realised what a fine panorama of fells opens up from its highest points. When I stopped to take a panoramic picture, I noticed that a very interesting cloud layer was billowing over Scafell, so I turned my attention to the peak. With a longer focal length lens, I captured this 'layer cake' portrait of the mountain, with alternating bands of light from the base to the top of the picture.

Suilven Broods, Scottish Highlands
This telephoto shot gives an almost end-on view of one of Scotland's best-known mountains. The majestic shape of Suilven deserves a bigger impact than if I had taken it on a wider angle lens with too much surrounding scenery.

Ben Vair from Stob Coire Nan Lochan, Scottish Highlands

Certain kinds of landscape are, in photographic terms, timeless, and unchanging mountainscapes often fall into this category. This photograph is over 40 years old. It was taken in January, 1968 on my second-ever visit to Glencoe. I was on a winter climbing course with Hamish MacInnes, and our party had ascended 'Ingrid's Folly' on Gearr Aonach and proceeded to the summit of Stob Coire Nan Lochan with a huge sea of cloud below. I wouldn't say anything looks much different 40 years on. The same cannot be said for any number of glaciers I have photograhed abroad since 1968.

Above Pencelli towards the Black Mountains, Brecon Beacons

This scene in the Brecon Beacons National Park is in complete contrast to the rugged and steep mountain walls of Glencoe. Pastoral valleys lead to fenced or hedged enclosures as you gain height. The photograph looks over a lead-in fence, balanced by a tree, to the Black Mountains beyond, which are caressed by valley fog in a temperature inversion.

Snowdon from Moel Eilio, Snowdonia

With little interesting forground to use on Moel Eilio, I decided to risk the battered fence as a foil to the cloud boiling up the flanks of Snowdon beyond.

A great day on Striding Edge, Lake District

Although the figure is heavily clad in winter gear, somehow his thankful look upwards into the sun gives a sense of joy to the occasion, for about 30 minutes before this was taken, the sky was overcast. The weather broke up into glorious sunshine speckled with cumulous cloud and giving a superb clarity of atmosphere. The wide angle lens gives some dynamism to the ridge, and is used from a slightly different angle than is normally photographed.

Striding Edge, Helvellyn, Lake District

These two shots of Striding Edge couldn't be more different. Here, on a February day, there were over 100 people on the ridge above a temperature inversion, yet I was lucky enough to isolate two of my companions. I yelled at them both, the nearest to look at the other, who had kindly obliged and perched himself on a small pinnacle. Seconds after this one and only shot was taken, the cloud rolled over the top of the ridge and didn't lift again. Notably, it became my first published picture in 1980, a postcard for which I was paid a princely one-off fee of £20 for the UK postcard rights. Just as well I made a poster of it later, which sold several thousand copies in Lakeland over a number of years. Even after the millennium, the postcard was still on sale in Patterdale! Why didn't I insist on royalties?

Frozen tarn on Drysgol with Cadair Idris beyond, Snowdonia

The top of Drysgol in the Arans reveals fine and extensive mountainscapes for almost 360 degrees. A small tarn lies off the path to Aran Mawddwy in a shallow hollow below Drysgol and it is from here, with its surface frozen, I photographed this wild scene. The tufts of russet grasses make a line which directs the eye to the tops of Cadair Idris in the background.

Ice patterns in tarn on Drysgol, Snowdonia

I never leave a photographic location without making two checks; one to look around to see that I have picked up all my photographic accessories, and two, to take a final look at the scene to see if I might have missed something. Here I saw some attractive patterns within the ice, particularly at the edges of the tarn. Mountain photography need not be all about dynamic views. Within these wild environments, it makes a change to show some close-up details of the workings of the elements. The shapes remind me of clouds with silver linings.

Little and Large, (rock and Pen yr Ole Wen), Snowdonia

Anywhere around Llyn Idwal provides classic mountain surroundings. On the opposite shore to the Idwal Slabs, I noticed a rock which echoed the shape of Pen yr Ole Wen behind. I duly photographed the rock and mountain with foreground, background and sky. Seeing a shot is the photographer's benchmark. Coming in close to the rock , I used a very small aperture for long depth of focus, and repeated the shape of a portion of the rock with the dark mountain behind. The rock has miniature rifts and gullies scarred into its face, and highlights the difference in scale between itself and the mountain behind.

Glacial Erratic, Gritstone on Limestone, Norber, Yorkshire Dales

At Norber, near Austwick, there is a large field of rocks, which on closer inspection turn out to be gritstone boulders perched on limestone clints. This is the result of glacial activity, where the younger rock, the gritstone, has been transported by a former ice sheet from one place to another, coming to rest over the older limestone. I have been there two or three times, but only on this occasion was the light good enough to photograph. This example has been given a low angle, accompanied by the bonus of a great billowing white cloud behind.

Tryfan from Moel Siabod, Snowdonia

This and the next photograph are examples of how the British mountain atmosphere can conspire to give an almost painting-like quality. The colours look somewhat pastel, or perhaps even watercolour, with a slightly subdued, yet effective, light.

Scafells from Yewbarrow, Lake District

The composition concentrates on the many foreground stones which have been piled up to make the summit cairn of Yewbarrow. Scafell Pike, (left) and Scafell, (right) are the recognisable mountain shapes in the background, helped by the contrast of their dark shades against the light coloured cairn.

Crossing Sharp Edge, Cumbria

A mid-summer picture taken in the eighties when shorts really were short – as worn by the footballers of the day. Apart from this observation, the walkers are evenly spread out on this short but airy Cumbrian ridge, where the holds seem to be slanting the wrong way and a fall cannot be contemplated. Other walkers are seen on the flanks of the mountain below the exposed ridge.

River Duddon and Little Stand, Cumbria
Springtime blossom on two trees in Eskdale. The river gives an attractive
lead-in to the foreshortened mountain – Little Stand – which is decorated
above with white cloud. I would probably term this effort 'a pretty picture'.

Ben More Assynt and Elphin, Northwest Scottish Highlands

The A894 is a dream drive in scenic wonderland, flirting with mountain and sea. Up and down, and roundabout one goes, and if the weather is fine, this stunning area would vie with anywhere in the world. Population is sparse, traffic is quiet except in the summer, and small, isolated settlements are man's only intrusion into this wilderness. Elphin is one of these, and from the long hill south of the village, there is a fine view of it backed by Ben More Assynt.

Glensheil Forest peaks from Stob a' Choire Odhair, Knoydart, Scottish Highlands
The view is inland along Loch Hourn, the head, Kinlochourn, just out of sight, is nearly
eleven miles away from the camera. Above this, Sgurr a' Mhaoraich is seen (well-lit),
Gleouraich and Spidean Mialach are in shade, right, with the South Cluanie Peaks and
peaks of the Kintail Forest and Five Sisters left.

Two winter walkers west of Carn nan Sac, Glenshee, Scottish Highlands
This picture gives a kind of 'into the void' feeling. The Glenshee highlands
generally appear as billowing green, heathery hills in summer, but are
transformed in winter when under a covering of snow. The weather was
doubtful, but there was just enough light in the right places to enhance the
picture, with the walkers' tracks providing a lead-in.

Winter squall, Glenshee, Scottish Highlands

The view is from Carn a Gheoidh (975m) towards the knob of Carn Bhinnein (917m) with the larger bulk of Glas Tulaichean (1051m) behind. I noticed the way the leading squall cloud curved menacingly over the summits, to be followed a short time later by complete envelopment by the mass of weather behind it (right). Although the foreground was flat, the intervening shapes of the rocks helped to fill it in.

Evening, High House Tarn, Glaramara, Lake District

I had climbed Glaramara from Rosthwaite and beyond the top, between it and Allen Crags, I bivouaced on the right of the tarn's horizon as seen in the picture. Before I did this, I obtained some pictures of the tarn in the low light of a long evening in early June. To frustrate me, the sun had been out until I got to the summit area, but then it hid behind a large bank of cloud to the northwest. Later, it was just powerful enough in its last embers to put some colour into the rock bastion which guards the left of the lake, and reflect in it some attractive cloud above the Langdale Pikes.

Dawn and cloud line over High House Tarn, Glaramara, Lake District
Complementing the last picture, this image again came after some frustration with the light at the start of the next day. A large bank of cloud had blocked a sunrise, creating a flat scene. However, patience turned out to be a virtue when I saw the cloud receding to the south. As it did, and the sun gained height behind it (beyond the left edge of the picture), the rim of the cloud took on an attractive shape. The calm lake was a great reflector of the cloud, hence the effect of the silver lining was gained.

Strange cloud streak off Suilven, Scottish Highlands
Those who know Suilven will recognize its western end buttress, as the summit of the mountain spews off a long streak of cloud to the east. Behind it a morning sun creates a glow. I cut the image down to letterbox format to include the one (important) sheet of water, and to accentuate the strange cloud effect.

Liathach and Ben Eighe from Beinn Bhan

So frustrating was the weather, I visited Applecross on three consecutive days in an almost hopeless quest for photography. On the third attempt, although the sun didn't get through, I walked to Beinn Bhan from the Bealach na Ba on the Applecross peninsula, and felt I could gain something from a telephoto shot using the drawn-in intervening ridge of Beinn Damh as a foil to the Torridon peaks beyond. It is at least moody and somewhat graphical, proving flat light can work occasionally.

Cloud boiling over Stac Pollaidh, Scottish Highlands

The *contra jour* effect on the cloud gives an impression that there has been an explosion of catastrophic proportions. The primeval end-on shape of Stac Pollaidh adds to the result.

On the Castle of the Winds with Snowdon beyond, Glyder Fach, Snowdonia
When you are on the mountain tops in mid-week, you can still encounter others, to whom in this case I shouted to perch themselves right on top of the Castle of the Winds, a stunning rock-shattered formation between the two Glyders, Fach and Fawr. A nice moment, giving a true mountaineering feel to an end-of-day scene. Very soon the couple were scampering down the Gribin ridge to the valley, while I stayed aloft on the mountain to bivouac near the summit of Glyder Fach.

Last Light over the Nant Ffrancon valley, Snowdonia
As for the previous picture, I stayed alone up on the Glyders and, in the last throes of light, saw the Nant Ffrancon river snaking down its classic 'U' shaped valley towards Bethesda. The beams came across and struck the flanks of Pen yr Ole Wen while the Menai Straits were included to create a lateral block to the top of the picture. I was pleased with the minimalistic result.

Climber on Meall Greigh with Ben Lawers behind, Scottish Highlands
It would be a long undertaking to traverse the whole of the Ben Lawers range in one winter's day. Instead, members of my mountaineering club opted for two separate excursions. The first main peak climbed was that of Meall Greigh. From near its summit, one of our taller members plodded downhill, and, silhouetted against Ben Lawers, his posture somehow put over the strenuous effort required. Ben Lawers is the ninth highest mountain in Scotland, and while it hasn't a particularly spectacular outline, it certainly puts over its large presence in the background of this picture.

On Pen y Fan, Brecon Beacons
A lone climber looks out in sunshine over the cloud-filled void which reveals part of the Brecon Beacons ridge of Waun Rhydd, when winters really WERE winters!

On Moelwyn Mawr with Nantlle Ridge behind, Snowdonia
On an early July evening with a view to bivouac on Moelwyn Mawr,
I saw an opportunity to use my companion, with the fine outline of
the Nantlle Ridge behind a series of tonal spurs.

Glassthwaite How & Ullswater, Lake District

Nothing beats the Lake District for autumnal colours. From the slopes below St. Sunday Crag, stunning views appear over Ullswater as the lake bends left to right. However, I noted the possibility of zooming in to the detail of the valley floor, where the white building of Glassthwaite How is prominent. The trees, bracken, and pastures are lovely greens and browns. There are one or two boats on the lake which provide scale.

A5 overlook from Tryfan North Ridge, Snowdonia

Nowhere else in Britain's mountains does a major trunk road hug up so closely
to an individual mountain as the A5 does to Tryfan. Climbers can get more or less
straight onto Tryfan from the A5, and even at this photographic viewpoint, which
is less than half way up, there is a fascinating overlook, not only to the figures but
to the string of tiny cars parked on the road below. Llyn Ogwen is to the left.

Looking East from Plynlimon, Central Wales

For one of the principal mountains in Wales, Plynlimon does not support big cliffs, major buttresses, or even a well-defined summit. But what is does have is bulk and remoteness. Much of its make up is moorland, with the sprawling Hafren Forest to the east, and it would be easy to get lost up there in mist. I have crossed it on the 45-mile Across Wales Walk on seven occasions, and been to its summit at least two further times. This was the only snow I ever experienced on the mountain, and I used the fence as a lead-in to the secondary top, Pen Plynlimon Arwystli, to the east.

Llyn Lluncaws & Moel Sych, Snowdonia
I have often journeyed into less fashionable mountains seeking differences in terrain and settings. The lonely Llyn Lluncaws is a solitary glacial lake beneath the long, broad Berwyn ridge, photographed here on a typical Welsh day, when the weather couldn't make its mind up what to do.

Summit Rocks, Esk Pike & Langdale Pikes, Lake District
As the sun went down on Esk Pike, I focussed on the colour-rich
rock detail of Esk Pike's summit, using a small aperture so that
the Langdale Pikes were relatively sharp in the background.

Iced Rock, Arennig Fawr, Snowdonia

Nearing the summit of the Arennigs on a fine cold March day there was a smattering of snow, but, more interestingly, lots of hoar frost and water ice on the walls, fences and summit rocks. It had been sculptured by high winds, and the freezing calm of the night before had held it in place. I noticed that this particular formation looked like the skeleton of a bird, and I concentrated on this as the main subject. It is possible to pick out Snowdon in the far distance.

Sugar Loaf & The Black Mountains from Skirrid Fawr, Brecon Beacons

Although Skirrid Fawr, (true name, Ysgyryd Fawr) falls short of 500 metres, it nevertheless feels like a proper mountain, with a seemingly lofty elevation. Yet it is easily reached from surrounding roads and lanes, and gives fine vistas across the Garenni and Usk Valleys to the surrounding hills. Abergavenny's Sugar Loaf (left) is a conical hill from most angles, providing a bold statement to the end of the Black Mountains, from which it is separated on all sides by deep valleys. Note the lovely clouds decorating the skyline.

Langdale Pikes from Brown Ghyll, Lake District
The two foreground rocks were selected because of their similarity to the shapes of the Langdale Pikes behind. The dramatic foreground light contrasts with the foreboding background.

Yr Elen from Carnedd Ucaf, Snowdonia

Yr Elen is out on a limb of the Carneddau main ridge. To climb
it, particularly if doing 'The Welsh Three Thousanders' one
has to go out and back from the main ridge almost two miles
return. I have included foreground rocks at a similar tilted
angle to the right hand ridge of the mountain.

Summit cairn, Pike o' Stickle, Cumbria

The slopes beyond the cairn were fairly boring, so I used the stones as a graphical foreground to the looming Skiddaw in the distance. The atmospheric conditions were such that a watercolour quality comes through in the picture.

Crinkle Crags & Bowfell from Pike o' Blisco Cumbria

The picture relies on the dramatic strong foreground light and the dark, etched mountain outline behind.

Looking at Garbh Bheinn, Scottish Highlands

February 1994 saw a very hard winter in the Lochaber Highlands, and it is very rare these days to be on the Ardgour Peninsula and find Garbh Bheinn in such Arctic conditions as shown here. As stated before, the mountain falls just short of being a Munro, but its grand structure gives the facade of something much bigger, particularly as the cloud lifted from its face to present this winter aspect.

Summit convergence, Carn Mor Dearg, Scottish Highlands
Sometimes inclement conditions break briefly to allow use of the camera. I was doing the classic Carn Mor Dearg/Ben Nevis circuit in squally weather, when I saw two climbers ahead just below the summit of the 4000 foot mountain, which was cloaked in snow. As they moved, the cloud parted, and I seized on the opportunity of the triangular shape of the peak with almost an inverted triangle of blue sky above it. There are two convergences; one the two climbers converging on the top, and the other, the shapes of mountain and sky meeting at an apex.

Cnicht in stormlight from Cwm Croesor, Snowdonia
Just up from the Croesor valley, I photographed Cnicht standing proudly against a darkened sky, with autumn trees in the foreground. Small mountain though Cnicht is, it is as pleasing to look on as much bigger peaks, either at home or abroad. Perhaps the only giveaway would be the ability of a good eye to catch sight of the tiny dot of a sheep grazing near its summit.

Shafts and shades, down Eskdale from Bowfell, Lake District

Bowfell has been a lucky mountain for me because I cannot remember an ascent where I did not get a worthwhile picture. Occasionally, changeable conditions provide something special, as here when, out of the cloud-filled sky, these sun rays (called crepuscular beams or 'God rays') spilled. The beams appear to radiate in this optical illusion. They are actually parallel, but have a perspective distortion like looking at a long straight road with an apparent vanishing point.

Howgill Fells from Hutton Roof Crags, Cumbria

This was the result of an early summer's sojourn to a fascinating hill with acres of tilted limestone pavement. It was a question of making the best composition of the varying tones of intervening land while including the outline of the Howgill Fells behind. Colour doesn't really matter here, the end-product could have been just as effective in black and white – but the colour tones tend pleasantly towards sepia.

Dawn from Swirl How, Lake District

I spent a night bivvying near the remains of a Halifax bomber which had crashed on the mountain with the loss of all of its crew in 1944. I slept peacefully, experiencing no ghosts. The following morning the expectancy of a fine dawn was hindered by too much cloud, which can happen in Britain, even under anti-cyclonic conditions. However, the light improved to an almost painting-like quality, and I was able to take this image of the view from Swirl How down Little Langdale with its tarn on the right, towards the Helvellyn range, where Fairfield dominates.

Erosion in ochre, Afon Elan, Powys, Central Wales

I was returning from Aberystwyth over the Cwm Yswyth mountain road in flat light, and stopped at Pont ar Elan to take a forlorn look at the river, not expecting anything to materialise. However, I remembered I had my flash gun and long lead to camera in the car. Taking up position on the water's edge, my flash sychronised with my slow-speed shutter and threw angled light onto an intimate piece of wilderness, with the milky water swirling through the ochre-coloured metamorphic rock.

Creigiau Eglwyseg design, Central Wales

I have always been impressed by the facade of Creigiau Eglwyseg, behind Llangollen. The limestone scarp is decorated by bands of cliffs and rocks, interspersed by trees clinging to the slopes. Rather than include a straight shot from the superb vantage point of Castell Dinas Bran, I chose this one, which is a statement of a part rather than the whole of the scarp, and shows its structure.

Looking East along The Grey Corries, Scottish Highlands

The Grey Corries lived up to their name as weather conditions gave a monochromatic result. This is satisfying as the terrain is arranged as almost sketch-like. The walker is ascending Stob Coire Easain, and due to his dark attire, I positioned him in front of a patch of snow, with Sron an Lochain behind. To the left, Stob Choire Claurigh is the central summit and highest in the chain.

From Mullach Clach a' Bhlair towards Sgurr Gaoith, Scottish Highlands
The mountains rising from Glen Feshie are very Cairngorm in character, in that once on top the walker is faced with either a sprawling plateau or a billowing whaleback. Here the only punctuation is the three mile distant Sgurr Gaoith, which forms a mini peak nearly 400 feet higher than the general surroundings. Inundation by mist in these areas creates obvious navigation problems.

Cumulous Cloud over Raise & Blencathra, Lake District

The buttress above Striding Edge provides a popular scramble to reach the top of Helvellyn. Just as it peters out to the broad ridge above, I took this shot, drawn to the isolated and fluffy cumulous cloud coming in from the northwest, which became the chief subject of the composition.

Storm Cloud, east-southeast of Craig Cau, Cadair Idris, Snowdonia
Another example of an interesting cloud. Descending the Minffordd Path from Craig
Cau, I spotted this typical stormcloud. Note its characteristic bubbly upper portion
supported by a flat base under which there is obvious precipitation. The two sheep
look kindly at the camera, probably because I whistled at them!

Arennig Fawr at dawn, Snowdonia

Once again, an early hours start from the Midlands saw me driving over the Berwyn mountain road from Llangynog to Bala. As I came downhill, I saw Arennig Fawr in front, complete with a dressing of snow, and a very interesting sky began to appear. I made an unscheduled stop near the hairpin bend to walk some yards down a track to find the best foreground to illustrate the valley mist, with the mountain glowing behind.

The Aran ridge from Bwlch y Groes, Snowdonia
On the same midsummer's evening I had photographed on Moel Llyfnant (page 150),
I drove in the dark to Bala and then up the Bwlch y Groes, the highest road pass in Wales.
There I slept out on the small car park in order to catch the sun's first rays on the flanks of
the Aran ridge. The use of foreground grasses provides a good lead-in to the distant ridge.

Looking over Dow Crag, Lake District
The following two pictures deliberately scale the climber or walker with the cliff on which they stand. Here, Dow Crag falls away impressively as the figure in blue dares to play on its edge.

On the North Peak of The Cobbler, Scottish Highlands

The shape of the Cobbler makes it a unique mountain. Although it lies in the company of higher peaks, its crags give it the best skyline in the area. There are at least two routes to the top, and to gain its true summit via a window in a large perched boulder requires a hairy scramble, where a fall shouldn't be contemplated. The North Peak, (illustrated) with a figure on top, is reached by a short easy scramble hidden around its rear.

View over Buttermere & Crummock Water from Robinson, Lake District
Intense morning sunlight strikes the lower fells as the view extends from
intervening hills as far as the coast, where some wind turbines may be detected.

On the Nantlle Ridge with Mynydd Mawr & Moel Eilio beyond, Snowdonia
The eye follows the foreground from left to right and then continues naturally left
again to the skyline, on which it follows rightwards. The whole Nantlle Ridge is a
tough excursion, with numerous ups and downs between mountain tops on an
entertaining switchback. Being on the edge of the main mountains, it affords good
views of many peaks, as well as vistas out to sea.

Blackmount and Buachaille Etive Mor from Creag an Fheadain, Scottish Highlands

The upper part of Glen Lyon contains mountains which look out both down the glen to the Lawers range and through a gap to the northwest, allowing sight of the Blackmount and Buachaille peaks. The sheet of water is the reservoir of Loch an Daimh. This area seems seldom photographed in books I've seen over the years, and is a pleasant image from an uncommon viewpoint.

West from Gleouraich, Scottish Highlands
Gleouraich is a Munro conveniently positioned by the roadside of Loch Quoich. As an outlier to Knoydart's fine mountains, it affords excellent views both into the 'Rough Bounds' and in this picture, to The Saddle seen on the right. To the left, Ben Sgritheall is in the distance, and the nearer Sgurr a' Mhaoraich (1027m) is fronted by Sgurr Coire nan Eiricheallach (891m).

Looking South from West Face of Aonach Mor, Scottish Highlands

Who needs the Himalayas? Sometimes a Scottish Highland winter can fill our senses with a splendour far beyond the true scale of our more modest mountains. Here, for example, a casual observer could be kidded as to where it actually was. The view takes in some of the Mamores and the Glencoe peaks. The foreground ice patterns are particularly attractive.

Chopper over The Ben, Scottish Highlands

From Aonach Mor, Ben Nevis looks magnificent in winter raiment, and a diminutive helicopter hovers just above its buttresses. It is no wonder that continental climbers have often visited Britain's highest mountain in winter to test themselves when these kind of conditions can be found.

Gairich reflected in Loch Quoich, Knoydart, Scottish Highlands
This 919m Munro is the first peak to catch the eye both approaching and
entering the wilds of Knoydart along Loch Quoich. Bright sunshine, classic
clouds and still waters combine to make this a memorable image.

Ben Sgritheall & distant Torridon mountains from Stob a' Choire Odhair,
Knoydart, Scottish Highlands

Clarity is a prime ingredient of good mountain photography. This example looks
north across the void of Loch Hourn from the perch of Stob a' Choire Odhair to
Ben Sgritheall and beyond to distant Torridan peaks, of which Spidean a' Choire
Leith (Liathach's main summit) stands out in the far distance.

Snowdon range from Craig Llyn Llagi, Snowdonia

This October morning saw a torchlight ascent from Nantmor, passing the white
farmhouse of Hafod Owen and through the woods to the open moor, where the light
was just enough to see my way. I plodded up to Llyn Llagi, a wild setting, and began to
see the possibilities of good early sunlight catching the Snowdon range. I pushed on,
out of breath by now, to the left of the lake up a steep grassy rake to emerge on the
top of Craig Llyn Llagi. Here I was in time to catch the rich, warm sunlight striking the
Snowdon group across the valley. The 'herringbone' cloud was a welcome addition.

Moel Hebog and Nantlle Ridge from Craig Llyn Llagi, Snowdonia
Photographic opportunities abound in so many places on or around Cnicht.
This one uses strong light and colour in the lovely view from the crag above
Llyn Llagi, which yields several skyline pictures in an almost 180 degree vista.

Fell Mood, Lower Man towards Blencathra, Lake District
This result was achieved by noticing the play of light which gave near shadow with two small figures, then highlighting the track from Lower Man to Whiteside Bank, where some walkers can be seen approaching its cairn. The final hill in highlight is Watson's Dodd, while Blencathra broods (left) and the much smaller Souther Fell (right) is also seen.

Brecon Beacons from Mynydd Illtud

Once again, dramatic light plays a hand. I planned a side trip to this open
moorland road west of the A470 where there is a lake and bird sanctuary. I had
seen the road on the map and hoped it would provide a good view across to the
Beacons. It duly did, and the strong foreground light on the grasses is a foil to
the peaks of Pen y Fan and Corn Du, looking wild and remote in the distance.

Keswick, Derwentwater & the Derwent Fells from Latrigg, Lake District

The mini-mountain of Latrigg provides an easily gained top from which to view classic Lakeland. I left my guest house in Keswick very early before driving up the lane which goes up the back side of the hill. From there, a short walk led to the top, and I took many photographs on this theme before driving back to Keswick in time for breakfast.

Latrigg & Skiddaw, Lake District
Here, Latrigg is seen brightly lit beneath Skiddaw's brooding presence.

Mirrored cloud, High House Tarn, Cumbria, Lake District
This is what happened as the cloud (seen on page 97) travelled south,
giving an equally compelling reflection with the Langdale Pikes behind.

Fuar Tholl & Sgorr Rhuadh reflected in Loch Carron, Scottish Highlands
Having left Torridon driving south to circumnavigate Loch Carron, I stopped at its upper reaches, and walked some distance to pick up this reflection of these two important Strathcarron peaks.

Carn na Caim & A' Bhuidheanach from The Fara, Scottish Highlands

I have stayed at Newtonmore over several winters. While the Western Highlands are my favourite area in Scotland, the Newtonmore region has given me some excellent days and pleasing images of numerous mountains. One such was The Fara, which just falls short of being a Munro. It is seen from the A9 at the back of Dalwhinnie as almost a whaleback. I have ascended it twice; once as a training climb for more extensive excursions on bigger mountains, and once on a superb day for snow, sunshine and views to other mountains. The latter was the case for the following two shots. Near the summit cairn were slabs and blocks of wind-sculptured snow. I was particularly attracted to this foreground, which gives way to the backcloth of hills on the other side of the A9, whose skyline and gullies form complementary shapes.

Along Loch Ericht from The Fara, Scottish Highlands
Turning about 90 degrees right from the previous photograph and a little further
along the broad ridge of the mountain, the view along Loch Ericht was enhanced
by this strangely beautiful formation of snow bosses sculptured by the wind. The
loch leads to the wild expanses of Rannoch Moor beyond and its surrounding
peaks. The two peaks to the far left are Ben More and Stob Binnein.

First Light on Cyfwry, Cadair Idris, Snowdonia

My idea had been to ascend the classic Minffordd Path on a summer's evening, take some photographs and sleep in the refuge at the summit of Cadair Idris, then catch the dawn from the same place. There was so much haze during my late afternoon and evening ascent, it wasn't worth taking a picture of anything on the whole route. However, there was always the morning, and this was one of a sequence of dawn shots from near the summit. In June, the sun is north enough of east to cast its first light on Cyfwry before anywhere else on the front of Cadair Idris. It was a lovely sight, captured here. I cropped the image down from full size to delete an unwanted sky, thus drawing greater attention to the buttresses of Cyfwry glowing pinky orange in the dawn light.

Last Light on Catbells, Lake District
On a balmy evening on top of Hindscarth, I wandered downhill some distance to photograph the last rays of sun catching the flanks of Catbells, where everything surrounding it had gone into shadow. The resulting bivouac on the mountain was spent on green grass near the summit on the calmest and warmest of nights.

Afterglow, Snowdon from Moel Llyfnant, Snowdonia

I drove the lane from the southwest end of Bala Lake into wild country beyond Dolhendre on midsummer's eve to find a short back way onto this unsung mountain. Sure enough it reared its triangular shaped head some three miles further, accessed at first by a vehicular track after which it was pretty much go as you please up the mountain. Its rather isolated position gave numerous photographic possibilities, the most dramatic of which was just after sundown, when I composed this picture of interlocking lines culminating in the pyramid of Snowdon, behind which the sun had set.

Fan Gyhirych at Dawn from Cribarth, Snowdonia
This photograph goes back to when I was commissioned to co-photograph *Snowdonia to the Gower* with John Gillham. The light granted me at first allowed this colourful, simply composed upright of Fan Gihirych. All too soon, the 'red sky in the morning' scenario kicked in, and the weather detioriorated. Cribarth is a limestone hill above 400m and a good viewpoint with some interesting foreground rocks.

Along main ridge, Cuillins, Skye
This is the view along the rugged Cuillin from Sgurr Dearg on a summer's evening.

A glimpse of Loch Avon, Cairngorms
A stunning winter's day on a walk between Ben Macdui and Cairngorm in the Cairngorms gave this factual, crisp look to the south over Loch Avon.

St. Sunday Crag Study, Lake District
These detailed snow formations on the flanks of St. Sunday Crag
as seen from Striding Edge just cried out to be photographed.

Aonach Beag revealed, Scottish Highlands
As the cloud broke over Carn Mor Dearg and Aonach Beag, the shapes
created by the snow and clouds were enhanced by some dramatic lighting.

On An Teallach, Scottish Highlands

My son and I did the complete traverse of An Teallach from south to north on a good day in May. I snapped him as he descended, with the majestic tops of this iconic Torridonian mountain beyond. It had been 30 years since my first ascent of the mountain, and a shot of An Teallach was simply a 'must' for inclusion in this collection.

Summit ridge, Cnicht, Snowdonia
Some yards before the summit of Cnicht is a small, off-set promontory with
a drop before the final top is reached. It gives a good angle and, with the
view to Tremadoc Bay, a sense of scale which seems far beyond its modest
height of 689 metres.

Looking at the Rhinogs from Moel Llyfnant, Snowdonia
This wild setting is only broken up between the viewpoint and the coast by the north-south line of the A470 trunk road. The four main peaks of Rhinog Fawr, Rhinog Fach, Y Llethr and Diffwys are seen right to left, with yet another Y Garn far left.

Llyn Hywel & Rhinog Fach, Snowdonia
The same day as the previous picture saw me descend Rhinog Fach to Llyn Hywel. Walter Poucher called this lake ' one of the jewels of Wales.' Its cradled setting beneath the buttresses of Rhinog Fach make it hard to disagree with his statement.

Cuillin Afterglow (from Loch Brittle), Skye
Both the horizontal 'landscape' (page 190) and this vertical 'portrait' composition of the Cuillin are included because both formats seem to work on the same subject, which involved stunning light from a setting sun behind the camera.

Cul Mor, Cul Beag and Stac Pollaidh from Lochan Buine Moir, Scottish Highlands

This location on the tiny winding Lochinver road is a good alternative to the popular views of the Inverpolly peaks where Suilven is included. The warm evening light and the blue lochan contrast with the yellow gorse. If any blur is detected in the gorse, it was because there was a strong easterly wind.

From Stac Pollaidh to Cul Mor, Scottish Highlands

This shot came from an October ascent of Stac Pollaidh which was under a slight cover of snow. The first time I ascended Stac Pollaidh was in brilliant weather during the drought in 1968. I had only a Kodak Brownie camera with me in those days, and was more excited about getting to mountain tops than taking good pictures. On this occasion, the weather was decent without being too great for pictures.

First Light on the Central Fells from Swirl How, Lake District

Just before I took this image, the light was really flat. Then out came the sun, caressing an attractive line of foreground rocks and completely lifting the scene. I was also pleased by the etched effect of the mountainous line of the Central Fells, including Crinkle Crags, Bowfell and Scafell. Scafell Pike and company are in cloud, but the overall effect of this with the pastel coloured sky seemed to enhance the mood.

**Bleaklow Stones (including 'The Anvil'),
Peak District**
The location is fairly remote on the vast
expanses of Bleaklow. Just here and there
collections of rocks jut out of the skyline,
and Bleaklow Stones is one of them.
The composition was made by climbing
awkwardly onto some of the rocks and trying
to create a pattern. The Anvil is about four to
five feet high and is seen top right.

Rock Fingers, Glyder Fawr, Snowdonia

The picture edits two of seven shattered rock fingers which are upstanding some yards downhill from Glyder Fawr's summit. Snowdon can be seen between them.

Sphinx Rock, Great Gable, Lake District

Essentially, this is a record shot of this large perched boulder, seen from the Climbers' Traverse on Great Gable. It links with the previous image as an upright of a rock feature. The resemblance to the Egyptian Sphinx is remarkable.

Southwest Panorama from Meall nan Tarmachan, Scottish Highlands

A great Scottish winter's day saw me traversing the Tarmachan Ridge, in Tayside.
The sunshine felt like a summer's day in the Alps, and underfoot, the snow and ice
conditions were perfect. I selected this pristine view from Meall nan Tarmachan
looking at the intervening tops of Meall Garbh, the sharp peak behind the foreground
ice, and Ben nan Eachan. In the left distance are Ben More and Stob Binnein. The only
place seen in the picture which holds no snow is Glen Lochay.

Winter Panorama from Tarmachan Ridge, Scottish Highlands
A sister image with the previous one, only this time looking north.
Once again, both these pictures remind us that our mountains
compete favourably with any others in the world for scenic grandeur.

An Teallach seen from Inverpolly Forest, Scottish Highlands
The distant An Teallach is seen from the Achiltibuie road, beneath Cul Mor.
I believe certain British mountain views with their particular intervening
landforms seem to transcend their actual size, scale and place. Here, I
feel we could be looking at a mountain range in Tibet rising above barren
plateux or perhaps in South America rising above the alti-plano.

An Teallach from Loch Droma, Scottish Highlands

The sky was milky, but it gave a pink tinge to the overall effect of the photograph, gained from a carefully selected position along the shores of Loch Droma on the A835 Inverness to Ullapool road, where An Teallach reveals itself as a focal point at the end of the loch.

Moon over Cantilever Stone, Glyder Fach, Snowdonia

Never one to miss an opportunity, I took this several second exposure a few yards away from where I bivouaced for the night on Glyder Fach. This magnificent perched stone has been subject of untold picture-taking. However, I wanted to push the boundaries of photography to obtain an image which was different and memorable. With slow transparency film, there was a slight adjustment required to the ISO reading to cater for reciprocity failure. The rest was down to the tripod and a self-timer setting of a few seconds so that vibration was eliminated.

Evening Light over Llanberis lakes and Menai Straits, Snowdonia
A planned bivouac on Y Garn was baulked by an incoming weather front. Besides,
Y Garn has a shallow cairn and is very exposed to the elements, so only the calmest
of nights would have been safe here. However, before scuttling down the ridge to
bivouac at Llyn Clyd, I was able to record this image as the weather began rolling in.

Red Deer Portrait, Loch Quoich, Knoydart, Scottish Highlands

Near the road bridge along the loch which gives the view of the South Cluanie Ridge are one or two deer feeding posts. I have been there in October and again, here in April, and it has turned out to be an easy spot to photograph perhaps Britain's largest and most stately wild animals. It is possible to come within feet of the deer, and they are obviously used to people stopping and viewing them. All that is required is a decent zoom lens and a steady, quiet, unruffled approach without any sudden movement.

Lone Swaledale sheep and Blencathra, Lake District
As well as the native Herdwicks of the Lake District, white-nosed Swaledales are seen on many fells, as here not far from the top of Robinson. The picture focuses on the animal while Blencathra's out of focus shape, seen just prior to sunrise, still identifies the mountain to the trained observer.

The Rivals from Y Garn, Snowdonia

Just before the evening light turned sour, I obtained this softly-lit shot from Y Garn's summit looking over intervening hills to The Rivals on the Lleyn Peninsula.

From Fan y Big towards The Black Mountains, Brecon Beacons
Another area I have often been lucky to visit in fine conditions is the Brecon
Beacons. On several occasions I have traversed the range from Pencelli to
Storey Arms in December with the West Bromwich Mountaineering Club. I
have seen cloud inversions twice on these excursions as seen here, with the
Usk Valley blanketed in mist while the uplands bathe in sunshine.

Glencoe Peaks from Sgurr Mhic Eacharna, Scottish Highlands
This is the end of the tops on the Garbh Bheinn circuit. There was just enough light and clarity to show the Glencoe peaks popping up out of the valley mists. From here it was a steady descent to the valley.

Retreat from Garbh Bheinn, Scottish Highlands

The hard ice conditions from this tremendous day on Garbh Bheinn are seen to advantage in this contra jour image. The figure, with ice axe, paces down the slope whilst the sun glistens above the icy peak. Though not a 'Munro' Garbh Bheinn gave a particularly testing winter descent on the right hand flank seen in the picture.

Morning, Central Fells from Robinson, Lake District

I was attracted to the warm morning light both on the foreground and on the Central Fells beyond. The low sun again lifts the shot from what might have been just a record when the sun had gained enough height.

Dawn from Bowfell towards Skiddaw, Lake District
The sky was developing a pink colour as the pre-dawn light increased. I looked out over the Cumbrian Mountains and selected this composition as one of many. Skiddaw is shaped and positioned to look its best from many places from its western arc. It has been photographed from here many times, but not so many have seen a dawn as pretty as this.

Bla Bheinn from Loch Cill Chriosd, Skye
Most pictures of Bla Bheinn are taken from Loch Slapin, but on the journey from Broadford is the pretty Loch Cill Chriosd, from where this shot was taken, using attractive reeds as the foreground.

Ben Stack, Sutherland, Scottish Highlands
Yet another isolated and seldom photographed mountain which juts above the rugged Lewisian gneiss landscape of Sutherland. Distant views suggest it is higher than its 718m. On closer inspection, as here from the River Laxford, it appears less of an obstacle to climb, but nevertheless retains its conical shape and reveals attractive rock terracing.

Scafells from Three Tarns, Lake District

I chose an upright shot in clear, cloudless morning light, where detail was the key. Three Tarns is a distinctive and attractive spot set between Crinkle Crags and Bowfell, where the two Scafells oblige as a bold background.

Shade on Creise, Light on The Buachaille, Scottish Highlands

It takes time to discover the best places along the A82 from which to easily access two mountain streams which make up the River Etive. What is required then is early morning light and some atmospheric cloud conditions. The two mountains here, Sron na Creise, (the end of The Blackmount) and Stob Dearg (Buchaille Etive Mor's summit) are complimented by shade and light respectively. The wide angle view allows the sweep of water to lead in to the mountains.

God Beams, Saill Garbh, Quinag, Northwest Scottish Highlands
The A894 climbs the pass between Glas Bheinn and Quinag. As I drove over it,
I noticed the crepuscular (God) beams dropping over the precipices of Sail Garbh.
Pulling over to photograph, I very carefully stopped down the exposure with closed-
down aperture and obtained this satisfying almost monochromatic result.

Cul Beag Mood, Scotish Highlands

This *contra jour* telephoto shot of Cul Beag makes it look gigantic when seen here from the west. Again, I was looking at careful composition to include some foreground layers. The ascent of this mountain and Cul Mor is a tough proposition as the ground between them falls away to great depth, and careful route-finding is required so as not to get caught in the numerous sandstone cliff terraces in the descent of Cul Beag.

Liathach (evening from above Loch Torridon), Scottish Highlands

I am always impressed by the views from the road from Sheildaig to Torridon, and I had pre-selected this location many moons ago, but just needed the right evening to get the shot. Not only does Liathach rise virtually from sea level to nearly three and a half thousand feet, but its architecture is truly mountainous and its western top, Mullach an Rathain, 3358 feet, (1023 metres) viewed here, is hardly a junior to the higher eastern peak of Spidean a Choire Leith, 3456 feet (1055 metres). It was graced on this occasion with sunset light and pink cloud. The foreground rock leads the eye to the mountain over the loch.

Morning cloud cap on Liathach Scottish Highlands

Loch Clair is the classic viewpoint for Liathach. The walk from the road is barely more than 250 metres to obtain this stunning view. Again, I was photographing a well-known scene, but looking for extra elements. The April sun rose to shine down Glen Torridon. The mountain often wears a cloud cap, and like much greater peaks such as the Eiger, Liathach creates its own micro climate. The base and surrounds were warming in sunshine while the lofty ridge remained dank, dark and cold, but of great interest to the discerning photographer, particularly when the view is reflected in a calm loch as here. Its pink cloud cap adds a mysterious otherworldliness that is such a plus point in landscape photography.

East from Gleouraich, Knoydart, Scottish Highlands

I was attracted to the shapes of the snow in the foreground, and married these with the natural line of the ridge towards Spidean Mialach, the snow peak behind. Beyond that, other snow-covered peaks grace the horizon.

Sunrise over Tryfan and Carneddau, Snowdonia
The use of a 24mm wide angle lens and a graduated grey filter helped
this image. Consequently, the rising sun looks small in circumference,
but the atmospheric conditions and colours were superb. I was
positioned near the top of the Gribin Ridge near Glyder Fach.

Goodnight Cuillin, Skye

From Glen Brittle campsite a gate gives a path to a suspension bridge which can be crossed to a collection of three cottages with the name of Bualintur. Passing these, I accessed the beach on the outflow of the River Brittle, where the clear crisp air gave superb clarity and colour as the sun sank out of sight behind me over the hill. I picked a suitable foreground, hoping that the mountains surrounding Coire Lagan behind would begin to take on a warm glow. I was stunned, however, by their superb rich colour, accentuated by an attractive pink, almost red, cloud hovering above them. The choice of the foreground of rippling sands and stones was a highly satisfactory decision.

INDEX

ACKNOWLEDGEMENTS

I should like to dedicate this book to my lovely wife, Pauline, who supports me in my photographic exploits without condition, particularly when I've disappeared overnight or for several days in my pursuit of this book and other projects, or even weeks when it has come to trekking the greater ranges of the world.

I am also very grateful to the friendliness of the West Bromwich Mountaineering Club over many years, despite the fact that I am only able to attend outdoor meets very spasmodically. Numerous images in this book, however have been shot on those meets I have been able to attend.

I would like to thank Roly Smith who, in reality, kick-started my renaissance in photographically illustrated books, and was behind five regional titles I did over recent years with another publisher, and has also had a hand in this book.

Finally, I would like to dedicate this book to anyone who appreciates the beauty of mountains, particularly those of our homeland, and when not physically among them, hopefully, they will be looking at this offering and be there in spirit!